A Glimpse of Heaven

A Vision of Eternity In A Moment of Hell

Peter-John Courson

Dedication

To my dad, who sat by my hospital bed every single day

Contents

Forward

It was one year ago today,

I had just released the last book "It Is Finished".

I published the wrong copy.

One that was unedited.

What was I thinking?

I wasn't.

I had bacteria growing in my brain.

My brain was literally melting down.

I was being operated on at nearly the same time I had published that book.

Needless to say, I have a different strategy for this one.

As soon as I hit "publish" I am going to thank the Lord for my health.

Then I am heading to In-N-Out Burger rather than the Rogue Valley Hospital.

Having established that,

Here is why I wrote this book.

While in the hospital I had a vision of Heaven.

Literally!

My personality isn't very flamboyant.

I am not necessarily a charismatic kind of guy.

I simply believe that our God has a wonderful sense of humor.

That is why He gave this down-to-earth guy a vision of Heaven.

Perhaps there is Divine kind of "last laugh" out of all of this.

Now, you may doubt I had this vision.

I wouldn't be offended at that.

Or think I was on too many hallucinogens,

At that, I would be offended!

But I know what I saw was Divine.

However, even if it was not a vision from the Lord,

What I saw is found in the Bible.

It is a vision stated in my own words.

But better than that...

It is confirmed in His Word.

So you can take it for what that is worth.

As for me, I simply state this:

What I saw is worth more than this world could ever offer.

Therefore, it has changed my world.

And I pray it may just affect yours as well.

I believe that is why the Lord gave this to me.

Chapter 1: "Introduction"

It was the worst.

It was the greatest.

It was the experience of my life.

I was given a vision of Heaven.

So much of this comes from my gut... Literally!

It was during the surgery on my stomach that I saw Heaven.

Like you, I've seen my share of potholes in the road of life.

Through all of that I had never felt like I was in Hell.

Until the month of August.

Until around my fortieth birthday,

I will not say I literally went to Hell.

(Praise the Lord)

I'll call it a Hell on Earth.

Happy birthday!

It was something I would never wish on anyone.

Not even upon my worst enemy.

And yet...

And yet...

When all was said and done,

Upon my reflection on the experience,

I might, just maybe, approve it for my best friend.

Going through Hell last summer brought me to Heaven.

A vision of Heaven.

I will even say it literally.

Until my last breath here I will be convinced of this...

I had a moment There.

Paul had a moment There.

And said it was beyond words.

The Apostle John had a Revelation of There.

And wrote of it in twelve thousand words.

By no means am I in the same category as those two!

I simply bring up that each responded differently to their vision.

My point is while Paul couldn't explain his vision of Heaven,

And John expressed his in detail,

I feel the calling of the Lord to go ahead and share of something of mine.

Chapter 2: "Take Me Out"

So here's the story leading to the vision.

(Edited for graphic content... for the most part)

I had taken my eldest two daughters to dinner and a movie.

Along with a couple of their teenage friends.

All of them truly engaging, intelligent young ladies.

I was able to act normal during the dinner.

But I didn't touch my food.

So I got a "to-go" box and we left the restaurant.

Note: Two weeks later my wife told me she found the box of food in my car.

I begged her not to throw it away.

She refused to bring it to my room.

That is how eager I was to escape the delightful hospital cuisines.

After dinner, the girls lovingly drafted me to a chick flick.

But I got out of it.

Not in a good way though.

It was the beginning of my trip to Hell.

And by that, I mean something even worse than a chick flick.

Instead of going in to theater I volunteered to get them some ice cream.

I was quickly spiraling down.

My stomach felt as though it was collapsing.

Or exploding.

Or something!

I laid down in the back of the car.

Somehow I made it through the time of the movie.

In the car they piled in.

I resumed acting as though everything was cool.

It was just a few months before that my daughters saw me in Critical Care.

My head had been operated on for Cerebral Meningitis.

For weeks, they saw me unconscious.

Or worse yet, speaking like a man out of his mind.

They wept as tubes were protruding from my head.

I wasn't going to allow them to see their old man suffering...

Again!

So I behaved manly and took them home.

Acting as though life was sweet.

It really wasn't.

It was awful.

At least, I was in an awful lot of pain.

I dropped off the ladies at our house.

They baked food.

I blitzed off.

I headed to my home away from home...

The Rogue Valley Medical Center.

A place where... "everybody knows my name".

A Glimpse Of Heaven

It's never quite a beautiful get-a-way.

But this time, it was especially painful.

It was an excruciating drive to the emergency room.

I didn't even tell my wife where I was headed.

I was over telling Amanda about all my health problems.

She has enough kids to watch without having to take care of this old man.

Again!

She is studying to be a nurse.

At least two of my daughters want to be nurses when they get older.

Either that comes from God giving them the heart of a servant.

Or it shows all that this guy has put them through.

Or... Both!

Therefore, Amanda wouldn't appreciate me ditching her.

But a chronically ill man has to do what a chronically ill man has to do.

So I went without telling her.

The concierge told me to wait in the waiting room with the other patients.

I decided to wait on the ground.

They asked me to get back up.

I told them I could not.

They set me in a wheelchair.

I fell out of the wheelchair again and again.

I would have preferred riding in a hearse at that point.

After some time, they figured I wasn't being dramatic.

Or vying for a fix of drugs.

They wheeled me into one of the patient rooms.

The time I waited there was longer than I could begin to explain.

Time drags when you're not having fun.

Finally, the doctor comes into the room and asks what is wrong.

I told him, "I have no idea!"

"All I know is I have a tummy ache."

So we decided to look at where all the pain was.

And we looked at my stomach...

Literally!

I had been diagnosed with Crohn's Disease when I was twenty years old.

Sometime later I was wearing an ostomy bag on my stomach.

Not many thirty-something year olds have to wear a bag.

But it sure beat lying in bed day after day.

Well, on most days...

Or some days.

The doctor wanted me to roll back the bag to look at the place

I was complaining about.

As I rolled the ostomy bag back, that is when I spilled my guts.

Literally!

My intestines fell out.

They fell out of my stomach and onto the ground.

I looked at the doctor and simply said, "Put me out of my misery."

He said he would,

And then bolted from the room.

Chapter 3: "God Had Told Me"

The doctor left me with an angel.

She was a young nurse who was holding both me and my stomach.

All my inward parts had been placed in a plastic container,

And set next to me.

She told me that the Jesus loved me and everything was going to be okay.

Later, I found out that 10 years before I baptized her in the amphitheater.

We do indeed "entertain angels unaware"

And then I was knocked out,

Along with my intestines.

I drifted off grateful to be anywhere but in conscious life.

I wasn't missing the Rogue Valley Medical Center.

That is when the Lord spoke to me,

Just as clearly as any one had ever dialogued with me before.

He is my Father.

He is my Friend.

He comforted me when I needed Him most.

The Lord told me two things in that moment of time:

First, He said that my intestines would be completely healed.

For the first time in years, they would be back into my stomach.

That would have been a grand miracle in and of itself.

But the best was yet to come...

Second, He told me that I would see Heaven.

It was made clear I wasn't going there as my final destination... Yet!

I would simply visit.

And take that message back here to my family.

To my church...

And to you.

When I regained consciousness, I saw my doctor's face.

It was an expression of pity.

He was virtually speechless.

He had no idea what to do with me at that moment.

As I was waking,

The doctor told me he just couldn't fit all my intestines back in my stomach.

His plan was to punch another hole

So that now I might have the privilege of carrying not one...

But two ostomy pouches on my stomach!

As enticing as it sounded to have as many tummies as an antelope,

I told the doctor that would not be the final outcome.

I told him, "Thus saith the Lord."

My poor doctor!

Being told by his patient to freeze in his surgical footsteps.

He shook his head.

I simply grinned.

What more could I say?

God had spoken to me.

As he was leaving for the surgical room, I called out to him.

"One more thing," I politely asked.

"Might you call my wife?"

Amanda may have assumed where I was located.

My usual hangout.

With my peeps.

At the hospital.

Now he would call her and confirm it.

The physician agreed to speak with Mrs. Courson on the phone.

I grinned.

Somehow I knew once he told her what he had planned to do,

My beautiful and (thank the Lord) demanding wife,

Would confirm what Jesus had spoken to me.

She was also in contact with the Great Physician.

She not only confirmed to him what the Lord had spoken to me.

She demanded it.

Amanda told the physician just what he would do.

He wasn't going to merely create another hole for my intestines.

I wasn't going to carry another bag.

According to her, he was going to place my stomach back where it belonged.

In my stomach.

The physician began to look edgy.

Nervous.

He was glaring.

And I was smiling.

The moment I had wanted to escape was soon to become...

The moment I'd never want to end.

The mask was placed upon my face.

I was surrounded by knives and scalpels.

But I wasn't in the operating room.

The medical team knocked me out.

The Lord had called me up.

Chapter 4: "Heaven is Fun"

I have never had so much fun in my life.

I smile just writing about it.

I've always known there is majesty in Heaven.

The Scriptures tell me of Heaven's glory.

There is no question concerning Its beauty.

But have you ever thought about how much fun?

When I was there, we were having not just a great time.

We were having the best time.

Ever!

It was as though it was magical flow,

Of God's people.

Dancing.

Together.

No one's eyes on another.

In my vision, we were busy dancing.

And laughing.

And singing.

We had zero moments to really analyze who was beside us.

No one person was the center of our attention.

But it sure was fun having them there though.

Make no mistake about that.

There was my mom.

I hadn't seen her for over thirty years.

She danced right beside me.

My sister died when I was a teenager.

Now I saw her dancing.

I always imagined I would one day see them in Heaven.

Never did I realize that we would be so busy dancing!

That is how it was when I was in the dance.

We all knew who was dancing next to us.

But we weren't staring at each other.

We couldn't analyze the situation.

We were simply in the moment.

There I was with David and Esther.

As well as Mary and Joseph.

Yep!

Noah and Enoch.

They were all around me.

Dancing!

I saw them, without looking at them.

No time to analyze.

How do I say this as respectfully as possible?

It didn't really matter who was dancing next to me,

At least in terms of being a part of the "in crowd" or not.

We were all having too much fun.

We had no time to be in awe of each other.

Or compare ourselves with one another.

To stop and analyze.

All we had time to do was to...

Dance!

There was no time to reflect on life.

There was literally no time for regret.

Crohn's Disease didn't enter my mind.

Gravesites were of another world.

No sorrow.

Nor nostalgia.

Not even reflection.

I have never danced in my life here on Earth.

Or at least, not well.

But now I see why people do it.

You can't look down.

You can't think back.

You are simply in the moment.

In Heaven, we were all in the moment.

Chapter 5: "The Dance"

On the horizon there was a citadel,

A building very simple yet beautiful.

It was transparent.

Completely see through from wall to wall.

Except where it wasn't.

In some places of the massive structure it was onyx.

Or agate.

Or something.

I still cannot say for certain what was within that citadel.

The gates were open.

But we never danced through.

The reason?

The Wedding has not yet started.

This was merely the warm up act for a coming attraction.

When He comes again!

We will all dance into the citadel.

When all have arrived.

When you get there!

I do not know what is within the citadel.

I do know Who is in it.

It is our Groom.

Our Champion.

Our Savior is awaiting His bride to dance within the city walls.

It will be the Wedding Feast of the Lamb.

Ever been to a grand wedding?

Even the greatest of those does not compare to That Day.

We will all be having so much fun.

Anticipation.

Someone Special is awaiting us within that citadel.

We won't have to analyze the situation.

Not for one moment will we even be able to take in the moment.

It was too gloriously overwhelming to pause.

And "take it all in".

Jesus stated in Heaven there is a woman.

She had been married seven times in her life.

Each of her husbands had died.

(What was she cooking?)

Jesus said it would not even matter.

That there would be no ex-husband factor.

How does one escape all the lifetime of drama we might have?

We will be too busy.

Dancing.

We will "remember ye not the former things" no more.

Chapter 6: "Fields of Gold"

The Golden Streets are not as you may picture them.

At least not how I did before I saw them.

We were dancing in a field.

Golden Barley.

Or so it appeared.

It was all around us.

It was up to my knees.

Those were the streets of gold leading to the citadel.

Yes, I know.

Upon reflection, I am aware.

Back in the 90's, Sting wrote a song about just that.

He wrote about dancing in fields of golden barley.

Perhaps the Lord was speaking through Sting.

Depends on if you are a Sting fan or not!

Have I mentioned how much fun?

I was so laughing on those golden streets.

I have mentioned how much fun, haven't I?

It's just that I could feel how perfect everything was.

The most expensive material here in this life,

Was simply fields to dance on in that life.

My worst day had become my best day.

And now I know that even on a good day...

The best is still yet to come!

Lastly, what I saw was a sea on the horizon.

John wrote in Revelation that before the Throne is a "Sea of glass"

Yet He also wrote that there is "no more sea" in Heaven.

What I conclude is the Sea led to God's Throne.

You and I need not wait until that day to dance before His Throne.

In Hebrews 4, we are told to "come boldly unto His Throne of Grace."

For what?

To "obtain mercy, and find grace to help in time of need." (Hebrews 4:16)

You can come to His Throne.

Right now.

For what you need.

Based on mercy and grace.

I don't know about you....

That makes me want to dance!

Chapter 7: "Crowns of Joy"

Paul spoke about crowns in Heaven.

So did James.

And John.

And Peter.

So it must be of infinite importance!

There is a Crown of Life for those who persevere.

In other words, for not giving up.

A Crown of Righteousness is ours as we look forward to That Day.

Just for wanting to join the Dance!

There is a Crown of Rejoicing for preaching the Gospel.

Simply sharing Good News.

A Crown of Glory for being faithful in service.

And a Crown of Incorruption is given to those who live for more than what is here on Earth.

Maybe even as you read this, you want to do just that

These are all found in the New Testament.

Personally, I did not see a crown on the head of a saint.

There may be literal crowns in Heaven.

I just didn't see it.

What I did see were people losing themselves.

I mean they were lost in joy and happiness.

That is why my own conclusion on Heavenly Crowns is connected to joy.

The crowns are not wardrobe accessories.

Nor are they anything material.

Not from what I saw.

Each crown was all about capacity.

To let go,

To step out.

To simply dance.

The ability to understand what Heaven truly is.

For some it will be a beautiful dance.

For others, it may be something...

Beyond words.

I cannot fully explain this.

I simply know that we can't get bogged down here on Earth.

Because soon, we will be dancing in Heaven!

Chapter 8: "My Mom is Dancing"

I was five.

I would be crushed.

The Lord would restore me.

But I would never fully recover.

My mom had died and went to Heaven.

That night I was sleeping on my bunk bed.

My dad walked in with a bandage on his cheekbone.

He was there with a group of people.

My uncles.

But not my mom.

The next day we drove to Coos Bay, Oregon.

That is where my Papa and Nana lived.

He took my sisters and I to his parents' house.

I do not recall wondering where mom was on that drive.

We walked on the beach.

My dad took Jessica, my sister.

He took me.

He told us that our mom was in Heaven.

That is when I first was fascinated with Heaven.

I wondered what Heaven was like.

"What is she doing there?" I asked him.

I've often thought about that.

Now I know.

At that time, I had a preschool teacher named Ms. Valerie.

She was and always will be my favorite teacher ever.

I hadn't spoken to her since I was one of her preschool students.

Just today, as I write this book, she sent me a note.

I do not think that is coincidence.

"I am not sure your remember me but I worked at Kiddie Corner when you and your sisters went there. I called you Torpedo John. I was working the day you guys were at the daycare and your parents had the car accident. All I could think of was why would a great God take such a loving mother from her children.

I always wish it could have been me so you guys could still have her. I used to go to your dad's church but after that it was too hard for me not to cry and wonder why He could not take me who had no children and let your mom live. I will never understand it. I was just as confused and bewildered why your family would have to go through the loss of your sister, too. I will say your mother was so wonderful. She loved you guys so much and she was stunningly beautiful. I loved you kids so much when I knew you. You were all so sweet, loving, and well behaved."

She wasn't the only person who thought me to be well behaved.

I am told that I was a sweet little boy.

I was respectful.

I was courteous.

I was a fine young man.

But only until my mom died.

Since then, I was not so well behaved.

You can ask any of my elementary school teachers,

Or blessed nannies and babysitters.

You can even ask my family.

I was just barely not a felon as a kid growing up.

I like to blame that on that my mom's departure.

Maybe I'm not (completely) justified in doing so.

I just feel a little relief when I do.

We all hope for a "Get Out Of Jail Free" card.

A mulligan on the back nine.

We know sin is sin.

We also live in a fallen world.

One that has car accidents.

And sickness.

We need God's Grace.

Not only do we need to share it.

We also need to receive it.

I sure do!

I was no angel as a kid.

More like a Tasmanian devil.

That is why I need God's Son.

Through Jesus, He has grace for all our sins.

Even if you are five years old.

Maybe especially then!

Chapter 9: "Good Out Of Bad"

Life is full of good times.

It also has its share of pain.

Like you, I've had my share.

Even before this vision of Heaven.

Earlier in the year I had spent six weeks in the ICU.

This was before my gut exploded.

On that occasion, my brain melted down.

I was out of my mind

The surgeons got into my head.

They removed the brain abscesses and saved my life.

It took me weeks to come mentally come back.

They suggested that I never would.

While I was recovering I provided some comic relief for my wife and my dad.

Good thing I was entertaining while out of my mind.

The Lord knows they needed it.

Directly following the brain surgery I preached the Gospel.

I have no recollection of the following conversation.

This is secondhand information.

I can only trust that it happened.

The name of the surgeon was Muhammad.

It was his job to gage where I was at.

He probed my mind.

He asked me who I was.

"I am a servant of the Lord Jesus Christ."

I preached the Gospel to Muhammad.

He shook his head.

My dad grinned.

Jesus was with me even when I was out of my mind.

For that matter, He still is!

Romans 8:28 states, "And we know that all things work together

For good to them that love God, to them who are called according to His purpose."

Everything is working together.

For the good.

His purpose rarely lines up with ours.

It is better.

That includes ruptured intestines,

And Cerebral Meningitis.

Not that all things are good.

Losing your job isn't necessarily "good."

A terminal cancer is not "good."

But God doesn't merely discard those things.

He redeems them.

He is able to take that mess in your home,

That pothole in the road of life,

And He will cause it all to be synced together.

God is able to make a beautiful work of art,

Out of a heap of hurt and ruin.

This past year, I've recovered from Cerebral Meningitis.

And I also have had my stomach sewn back up.

Lying in my hospital bed.

I never did say, "Thank You Lord."

Not that I remember, anyway.

But now I do.

I really do.

God will make good.

Even out of our bad.

He is able to make Good News.

Come out of bad times.

Chapter 10: "My Sister"

Jessica Leigh stood there by me that day on the beach.

She had lost her mom in a car accident.

It was thirteen years before hers.

From my perspective, not enough years before.

Growing up, unlike me, my younger sister was (virtually) faultless.

Jessica only was praised by her teachers in school.

She was loved by all.

She was talented, focused, and spiritual.

I was either the first or one of the very first to approach her crumpled Volkswagen.

The year was 1994.

I was eighteen.

I wonder what she would be like today.

It still hurts for me.

But not for her.

In Heaven.

She is not bummed out.

She is dancing.

She is not crying.

Nor hurting.

Not even recovering.

She is dancing upon streets that are golden.

A Glimpse Of Heaven

I can't bear to think of my teenage daughters behind the wheel.

My daughters shall never be allowed to drive.

I'm not joking!

(Though my wife may over rule me.)

As much as I miss my mom.

And my sister,

For a moment,

I danced with them.

Here on Earth, I am ever so gradually learning to dance.

Not literally.

I mean, learning to take this life less seriously.

To find that life is seriously funny.

Even among the pain and tears.

Because all that pain and those tears are going to be wiped away.

In Heaven, we won't even remember all the hell we had to go through.

As David danced before the Lord with all his might...

We are learning the steps of the dance,

As we keep our eyes on Jesus.

Chapter 11: "Grambo!"

Tammy Courson

She's been my mom since I was eight years old.

She put up with all my nonsense.

Except when she was all of 19 years of age,

She bent me over on her knee and spanked me.

I sure needed that spanking.

My two teenage daughters are in love with my mom.

She prays for them.

Talks Jesus with them.

My fourth grade twins are spoiled by her.

All four of my girls may as well refer to her as St. Tambo!

That is how good she has been for my family.

God is able to take my first mom's early departure to Heaven,

And bring to me a mom here on Earth.

He is able to have mercy on this wayward youth,

A belligerent, young punk,

And show me how to be a man.

All through a Godly mom.

A tender touch.

A wise woman.

St. Grambo!

Just writing these things is healing to my heart.

I am reminded it will all work out.

Everything you are going through.

All of it!

How do I know?

We have the eternal promise of being together.

With the Lord.

With each other.

Forever.

Chapter 12: "Finally Recognized"

I'm still hurting.

Some people see me as a pastor.

Others talk to me as a neighbor.

I appreciate the closeness of my family.

The graciousness of my church community.

And I am hurting.

Maybe you can relate.

Perhaps you are hurting.

In fact, more than "perhaps."

You have been hurt in life.

God knows.

Yet few others do.

No one can fully relate.

It may not even be anyone's fault.

At least, you don't seek to keep a tab.

You just cannot be fully recognized.

You will,

In Heaven.

As the Apostle John said in his letter.

"You will know as you are known."

You will find your place.

Fully recognized.

Though it may take some time.

Yet maybe for the first time.

When Jesus first rose from the grave,

Few people recognized Him.

Not immediately.

Not at first glance.

Mary Magdalene thought Him to be a gardener.

Peter and John saw Him on the shore.

They didn't know it was Him right away.

For Thomas to believe,

Jesus invited him to touch His wounds.

He traveled twelve miles with two of His disciples.

They finally knew it was Him once they sat down,

And broke the bread.

It took time but each follower would recognize Him.

Yet they would see Jesus in ways they hadn't before.

He was seen as He truly is.

Not simply as a carpenter.

Nor a mere rabbi.

Not even a healer.

He was seen as the Risen Lord.

When we are dancing on streets of gold,

I wonder how long it might take to recognize one another.

It might take some "time".

Not because we are hidden or disguised.

But we are finally seen for who we truly are.

All our masks are withdrawn.

Our flaws and sins taken away.

Maybe only in Heaven will we see.

Without all the junk.

No hypocrisy.

Simply love.

Chapter 13: "Heaven on Earth"

After my journey to Heaven, you'd think I'd be thrilled.

Yet in all honesty, a few days later, I was battling the blues.

I wasn't dancing anymore,

I was lying in a hospital bed.

The Lord reminded me that I wasn't in Heaven yet.

It wasn't only the Lord Who was reminding me.

So were the nurses,

And their needles.

Then I remembered my beautiful wife.

I looked at the pictures of my four gorgeous daughters.

I opened my Bible.

And I realized why we pray, "On Earth as it is in Heaven."

The Lord taught us to pray this,

That this life might be Heaven on earth.

The Kingdom of God revealed to us today.

On the Mount of Transfiguration were the "Big Three."

Peter, James, and John.

Initially, Peter wanted to build three tabernacles.

Then they saw "no man, save Jesus only."

Moses and Elijah had suddenly disappeared from sight.

My bet is that Elijah and Moses were still standing there.

Peter and the guys were just too focused on Jesus.

That is the key that unlocks the door to Heaven on Earth.

It is keeping our eyes on Jesus.

When Peter kept His eyes on Jesus He walked on the stormy waves.

Only when he was focused on the waves did he sink.

Keeping focus on his walk got him nowhere but downward.

What he needed to do was keep his eyes on Jesus.

Even in the storm the Lord gives His peace.

So that we might rise above it.

Even if it is windy.

Or stormy.

Or even feeling like Hell on Earth.

We simply keep our eyes on Jesus.

We take of His body and His blood.

We open His word.

We worship His Name.

And we take our eyes off our own walk.

The less I am taking inventory of my personal performance.

The more it is Heaven on Earth.

When I am taking inventory of me,

Or my situation,

In and of itself,

I'll drown in the waves of depression.

Perhaps that is what Hell will be,

People simply focused on themselves.

And in Heaven we will be lost.

In the joy of being in His presence.

Chapter 14: "A Sneak Preview"

The great, big irony in all this is that I didn't see Jesus.

When I was in Heaven I believe Jesus was on the Throne.

Within the citadel.

He was waiting for His Bride.

So what I saw was merely a warm up act.

It wasn't even the Main Attraction.

The mere anticipation of the Wedding.

That alone was the reason we had danced.

It was why we were laughing.

Jesus was in the House!

As fun as Heaven is, that is how awful Hell will be.

It will be awful not because God isn't there.

God the Father is everywhere.

Yet though Jesus is also God,

He will not be there.

And the absence of Jesus is what makes it Hell.

We see sneak previews of Heaven and Hell.

When Jesus is in the midst, there is the Kingdom.

It's a kind of Heaven on Earth.

In a home.

In a church.

In a nation.

When Christ is rejected,

Or pushed out to the margins,

Then what ensues is Hell on Earth.

In a home.

In a church.

In a nation.

I need Jesus.

So do you.

We need Him in the center.

We need Him as our Daily Bread.

While we wait for That Day,

You and I can experience Heaven this day.

It is as simple as making Jesus the center,

The reason we live,

And the way we think.

We can make Him the center through His Word.

By taking the Bread and the Cup in Communion.

Through worshipping His Name.

And by loving our neighbor as ourselves.

Those are the Kingdom.

That is Heaven on Earth.

Chapter 15: "Jesus Is The Way"

"I am the Way, the Truth, and the Life."

Jesus told that to His disciples just after describing Heaven.

"No one comes to the Father, except through Me."

There is One Way to Heaven.

The Gospel is that Jesus is the Way.

It is not my good works.

It is not your merit or behavior.

Jesus didn't come to Earth to point us in the right direction.

He is the Direction.

"By grace are ye saved through faith".

And even that faith?

"And that not of yourselves: it is the gift of God: not of works, lest any man should boast."

Have you received that gift?

Consider it the greatest invite you will ever receive.

To join the Dance.

Both forever.

And right now.

I want to know that you know that you will be in Heaven.

Dancing.

Having fun.

Forever.

A Glimpse Of Heaven

And I want you to have Heaven in your heart.

Today.

All you must do is believe.

It seems so simple.

That is because it is.

To enter that kind of Dance like the one that I danced in,

You must be as a child.

Philosophy will not save you.

Karma will not save you.

Religion will not save you.

Only Jesus Christ will save you.

He has already died for your sins.

He has paid the price.

Your debt to God is covered.

Simply receive it.

Simply believe it.

Chapter 16: "Live For Heaven"

"Live for Heaven and you will enjoy this world immensely."

You can find that quote on page 133.

The book is "A Place For You."

The subject is Heaven.

The author is my Pops.

Talk about knowing a thing or two about Heaven.

Saying a temporary farewell to his bride.

And then to his daughter.

Not to mention, his father.

That could possibly shake a man up.

Rather than that, those things have caused my dad to look up.

My dad is down to earth.

Especially, for being a "Southern Oregon Celebrity."

His life has not been easy.

But I bet he would tell you he has enjoyed it.

How?

More than any person I have personally known.

He has lived for Heaven.

After what I saw on my trip to Heaven,

I want to live for Heaven.

More than ever before.

And then I can enjoy this world, too!

Now...

Who wants to dance?

Made in the USA
San Bernardino, CA
30 November 2016